Also by Marian Head

Gratitude Journal for a Healthy Marriage (ebook) by Marian Head
— *Marlin Press: 2014*

Ageless Beauty, invited essay for *Click! Choosing Love One Frame at a Time* by Carl Studna
— *Hay House: 2013*

Suprasexual rEvolution (2nd Ed): Toward the Birth of a Universal Humanity by Barbara Marx Hubbard and Marian Head
— *Marlin Press: 2012*

Suprasexual rEvolution: A Radical Path to 2012 and Beyond by Barbara Marx Hubbard and Marian Head
— *Marlin Press: 2009*

The American Team: Seven Steps to Genuine Teamwork in the White House and Beyond, invited submission for the 1992 Presidential *Blueprint for Transition*
— *Marlin Press: 2008 (Rev. Ed.)*

VITAL Signs of a Healthy Business, invited chapter for *The Ultimate Guide to Network Marketing* by Joe Rubino
— *Wiley: 2005*

Revolutionary Agreements: Twelve Ways to Transform Stress and Struggle into Freedom and Joy by Marian Head
— *Marlin Press: 2005*

GRATITUDE JOURNAL FOR A HEALTHY MARRIAGE

*Gratitude saved my marriage
... and it may save yours, too!*

MARIAN HEAD

Gratitude Journal for a Healthy Marriage

Copyright © 2014 and 2015 by Marian Head
All rights reserved. Share freely and widely with your loved ones.
Acknowledgment requested and appreciated.

First e-book edition October 2014.
First print edition May 2015.

ISBN: 978-0-9839209-6-0

Layout, design, and cover created by Daniel Lane
www.PonoPhoto.com
Cover Photo by Daniel Lane
Marian & Glenn photo on page 85 by Daniel Lane

Edited by Stacey Stern
www.StaceyStern.com

Font is Times New Roman and Snell Roundhand

Marlin Press
2525 Arapahoe Ave. E4-133
Boulder, CO 80302

For my darling husband, on the 25th anniversary of our wedding day.

Table of Contents

Preface	6
The Journal	9
Day 1	14
Day 2	16
Day 3	18
Day 4	20
Day 5	22
Day 6-61	24
Revolutionary Agreements	82
About Marian and Glenn	84

Preface

During a difficult time in my relationship with my husband Glenn, I decided to write down one thing I appreciated about him every day. The process of focusing on what I liked about Glenn, instead of what I did not like about him, literally saved our marriage. He had no idea I was writing a gratitude journal — until I surprised him with it a year later, on our twenty-fifth wedding anniversary.

Five years later, Glenn suggested I publish the journal in the hope that it may help others struggling with their relationships. Although some of the entries are quite intimate, I agreed. The bulk of this little book is made up of scanned, handwritten pages from my journal.

I hope you will savor the unfolding love story as my relationship with Glenn transforms through this simple, yet surprisingly effective, process of daily journaling. Take your time. Linger on the journal pages that open your heart or stimulate you. Explore the types of behaviors that engender gratitude.

You might ask yourself:

- *Do I recognize these behaviors in people I know?*

- *Might I appreciate others even more if I focused on seeing the best in them?*

- *Do I want to embody any of these behaviors myself? Can I expand my own capacity to behave in ways that foster gratitude?*

- *When people express their appreciation for me, am I able to fully receive their gratitude?*

It is my hope that you will receive big value from this little book by asking yourself these questions.

The first half of my original journal is within the pages in front of you. I would be delighted to provide you with the second half of my journal one page at a time through daily emails, if you so choose. (For free and with no advertising!) Simply provide your email address at www.GratitudeJournalNow.com to let me know you'd like to stay in touch in this way. Trust me, the second half of my journal gets really juicy.

Finally, please share how journaling helps you transform your own relationships at www.Facebook.com/Head2Gratitude. Together we can educate and inspire others to build lasting relationships through the simple act of writing or speaking our gratitude daily.

With love and appreciation,

Marian

The Journal

The Journal

Have you ever met someone for the first time yet felt you've known them for a lifetime? That's how it was for Glenn and me.

We met as speakers at a professional conference in Montreal in 1981. At the time, I was Manager for Educational Development at the US Senate in Washington, DC. Glenn owned and operated a highly respected Colorado-based consulting firm. Because we were both leaders in the emerging field of computer-based training, he hired me on the spot. I began moonlighting for him that very weekend at the Queen Elizabeth Hotel. Although we didn't see each other again until the next year's conference, we developed a close friendship and deep trust as we worked together long distance.

A few years later, after each of our previous decade-long marriages ended for different reasons, we found ourselves exploring new dimensions of our relationship. As often happens with people who have been in less than fully satisfying marriages, we both yearned for deep connection. Our merging ignited a flame of desire and our passion burned hotly and steadily through our courtship and early marriage.

Six years later, just prior to my fortieth birthday, our precious son Michael was born. We moved into the next phase of our relationship with a good deal of humor at the loss of our previously ceaseless lovemaking and a respect for this new work together: parenting.

Even though we had come from different religions, political persuasions, and cultures (I from New Jersey and he a Texas Aggie!), Glenn and I were bonded through our ever-evolving work adventures and shared enthusiasm for personal development. Like most couples, we had areas of conflict, the most challenging of which were our different financial philosophies and practices. But all in all, we were doing fine — until 2008.

To describe 2008 as a really bad year would be an understatement. Like many, we were seriously injured by the financial debacle. But it was the insult I added to this injury that put our marriage in trouble.

It began when Glenn assumed the lead role in a business I had built for more than ten years. While I was happy to be freed up to focus on my new book, *Revolutionary Agreements*, I was unhappy with how he was running our business. I did not like what he was doing— and even more so, what he was *not* doing.

I began to criticize him often. I felt frustrated and angry. If only he would do business *my* way!

My judgments about Glenn's lack of discipline, goal setting, planning, taking appropriate actions (the way *I* would do it), along with his focusing instead on what I thought were feel-good, unimportant processes with our team, were infuriating. He was having fun, and I wanted him to WORK. Even though he took our business to the next level, I didn't let up.

For nearly a year, I was on edge. And I wanted to push him over it!

On our twenty-fourth wedding anniversary, I received this message from my inner conscience, "Keep it up, Marian, and Glenn will walk out. He won't complain. He'll just leave."

As angry as I felt, I knew I did not want to cause my marriage to end. What to do?

Remembering the expression, "We teach what we need to learn," I consulted my own book! A full one-third of *Revolutionary Agreements* is about gratitude. On page 124, I had written:

> *Gratitude has to do with developing the habit of seeing what's right rather than what's wrong; of seeing the best in everything around us.*

I was challenged. How could I see anything through my blind rage? I was determined to find a way to turn my attitude around.

That morning, I went off to sing with the local Unity Church choir. Afterwards, when browsing through the crafts being sold by the Youth of Unity, I came across a small, blank gratitude journal. Perfect!

Pasted inside the front cover was this quote:

> ## Gratitude Journal
> *Gratitude unlocks the fullness of life. It turns what we have into enough, and more. It turns denial into acceptance, chaos into order, confusion into clarity. It can turn a meal into a feast, a house into a home, a stranger into a friend. Gratitude makes sense of our past, brings peace for today, and creates a vision for tomorrow.*
> ---Melody Beattie

Sounded good to me! I made a commitment to write down one thing about Glenn I was grateful for every day in this journal.

# Day 1

As soon as I awakened, my mind went to work. I picked up my new little journal and thought, "Where shall I sit each morning to write down my gratitude?"

I reentered the bedroom where Glenn was sound asleep and sat down in the rocking chair I had nursed our son in nearly seventeen years before. Yes, this was the place. It felt good to sit in that chair with a purpose again.

That first morning I sat and sat, rocking back and forth, not knowing what to write. I was determined to be authentic and not make up something just to fill the page.

As I gazed at the sleeping man I had loved with so much passion for twenty-four years (well, perhaps twenty-three of those twenty-four), the victim within began to soften. I kept repeating to myself, "What am I grateful for? What am I grateful for? What about Glenn am I grateful for?"

Finally something authentic arose. As you can see from my November 24th entry, I still wasn't ready to express my gratitude directly to Glenn. But I could be grateful to John and Harold (President of NSPI) who had each laid a path for me to find Glenn. I was grateful that our meeting was inevitable.

Nov 24, 2008

I am grateful
for the paths that
led us to each other

— John Buck, with whom
I rode the public bus from
Columbia to DC every Friday...
and who consulted in the ECM

— President of NSPE,
who said, in the hallway of
Montreal's Queen Elizabeth hotel,
" There's someone I want
you to meet..."

 Day 2

I sat in the rocking chair once again and watched my husband sleeping soundly in bed. After a few minutes, a smile crept across my face as I wrote my next gratitude.

What a leap from how I felt just the day before! More significantly, it was light years from how I had been feeling for months.

Nov 25, 2008

I am grateful for you holding me all night in your loving arms ♡

# Day 3

On day three I made a big decision. I would write my gratitude every day right up to our next wedding anniversary. Then I would give Glenn the gratitude journal as my surprise twenty-fifth anniversary present to him!

That was ambitious, but having this new focus made me happy.

Sitting in my rocking chair, I waited for some burst of gratitude to emerge. When that didn't happen, I turned the clock back in my mind and reviewed Glenn's and my day together the day before. I recalled one of our business events and smiled. That's it!

Day 3

I am grateful for the way you speak about me to others, with pride sparkling from your eyes ♡

# Day 4

On the fourth day, my gratitude flowed more easily. My morning discipline became something I started looking forward to.

What would emerge? How would I express my authentic appreciation?

Oh yes, this gratitude stuff really was working.

Day 4

I am grateful for
your thoughtfulness
xoxo

Day 5

Now I was on a roll. One day after another, one thing I was grateful for after another appeared more and more easily, slowly rebuilding and rejuvenating the relationship I had once known. I became lighter, more tolerant, less bossy (read "bitchy"), and more loving. Amazing.

Could this simple daily practice produce such profound results so quickly? Without asking Glenn to do anything differently, I was falling in love with him again.

Day 5

I am grateful for your ~~surprise~~ of accompanying me to church ~~this~~ week.

✡
♡

Day 6

I am grateful
for your
integrity

♡

Day 7

I am grateful for your kindness to your friends

♡

Day 8

I am grateful for your infinite patience with me, especially in the evenings when I am tired & irritable...

I love you.

Day 9   Mon, Dec 1 2008

I am grateful for your Willingness to handle all Mannatech ordering. Thank you! xoxo

Day 10

I am grateful for your generosity — in regards to money, time & Spirit

♡

Day 11

I am grateful that the recycles disappear frequently — you take care of things with such ease, and no need for acknowledgment. ♡

Day 12

I am grateful beyond any utterance every time you give me an orgasmic back scratch!

xoxo

Day 13

I am grateful for the example you demonstrate of self-acceptance, "I am what I am" and with no trace of vanity whatsoever.

I am in awe...

Day 14

I am grateful for the friendships that we share with ease, like the Bakers who we played with tonight ♡

Day 15

I am grateful for the music you love to play & for the times we have held hands while listening to Peter Kater play in our presence, like tonight at Nissi's... You are my DJ ♡

Day 16

I am grateful for the quiet, easy, drama-less way you juggle so many of life's tasks almost invisibly.

XOXO

Day 17

I am oh-so-grateful to awaken in my favorite spooning position with your arm around me + your hand lovingly cupping my breast — we were built for each other, and for that I am grateful!

Day 18
Dec 10

I am grateful for your unconditional support — it is truly remarkable, extraordinary uncommon like you —

Dec 11
Day 19

I am grateful for the special touch you have to make money appear from "outside the box" (ok - so you can also make it disappear, for which I am not so grateful :))

You are a magician!
I love you ♡

Day 20

I am grateful
for your caring and
protective ways, for
lifting the heavy things,
both physical & not.

Thank you for carrying
our luggage today as
we depart for Texas
to visit Liz & her
children. ♡

Dec 13
Day 21

I am grateful for
you honest authenticity,
never performing,
always being just who
you are...
  a deLIGHT

♡

Day 22

I am grateful for sharing this Spiritual path with you
Thank you for acknowledging the Divine in all beings
♡

Day 23

I am grateful for this day with your son's family. I feel closer to you, and it feels good. I love how Mason "recognizes" you; your essence, so similar to his dad's, your son.

I am grateful for the gift of your children + grandchildren in my life.

Day 24

I am grateful for your special spaghetti sauce — yum! Thank you for making the best batch yet today at GJ's house!

Day 25

I am grateful for your easy going manner which makes life with you a pleasure.

Thank you for being you.

Day 26

I am grateful for the ease with which you share meals with me when we are in a restaurant. Tonight we attended the CAP annual party at Five Spice + shared a whole sea bass in spicy bean sauce. Yum!
(Thanks for letting me order brown rice for us, too 😊)

Day 27   12/19/08

I am grateful for all of the times you answered "What do you do?" with "I pleasure my beloved."

Yes you do.

With love
♡

Day 28

I am grateful for how lovingly you offer your arm to walk me steadily across an icy patch ♡

Day 29

I am grateful for your joy in the morning. You are so pleasant to awaken!

♡ ... especially if I wake you in that ~~special~~ way.

Day 30
end of month 1
25th year of
marriage

I am grateful + stimulated by every lingering kiss.

Day 31

I am grateful for you handling all of our financial transactions, and doing so without drama (because surely there could be some this year!)

I love you.

Christmas Eve
Day 32

I am grateful for the precious time we spend together; today as you prepared the turkey & I I prepared the walnut rice dressing

all to be shared with our dear friends Ward, Steve, Bill, Peggy, Nicole, Lexi & Michael 🩷🩷

Day 33

I am grateful for the thoughtful gift you gave to me today - accompanying me on the hike of my choice in Kauai - ahhh... my favorite activity: being with you in nature ♡

Day 34

I am grateful for your ability to screen out my menopausal, Michael-induced, or fear-based moods, knowing that "this too shall pass" and I shall return as your beloved.

♡

Day 35

I am grateful for the easy way you follow my lead (except when we're dancing!)

Although your response has changed from your younger years of "ok" to your mature years of "yes dear" the sentiment feels the same — Loving ♡

Day 36

I am grateful for your unwavering confidence in me. "Why don't you just write some articles & get them published?"

— especially when I am doubting my own abilities...

You are my greatest supporter, encourager & fan... + for that I am grateful ♡

Day 37

I am grateful for the ease you personify in all that you do. Perhaps it is a sense of unattachment that makes you so drama-less. You are so EASY to live with!

Thank god.

Day 38

I am forever grateful for your role in parenting Michael — from his conception in Moscow to our conversation during the walk in Pinebrook Hills when we talked about the responsibility of having a child to providing your unique loving perspective all of Michael's 18 years of life. ♡

Day 39

I am grateful for your love of women & the childlike joy you radiate when surrounded by us.

:)

Day 40
Jan 1 2009

Happy New Year!
I am so very grateful for awakening in your loving arms on this first day of the year of Hope & Transformation.
I Love you.
♡

Day 41

I am grateful for your willingness to try new things today, rather than "killing time" while I had a pedicure & manicure — you joined me!

♡ :)

Day 42

I am grateful that you and I share meals together when we go out to eat. You are so easy! ♡

Day 43

I am grateful for your ~~gentlemanly~~ ways — how you always lift the heavy luggage & care for me in so many small, yet meaningful, ways.

♡

Day 44

I am grateful for our deep spiritual connection. When I asked you, "What would you like to do on Kauai" you said, after a moment of reflection "Take a deep breath."

Then, in the intuition program I am listening to, I was asked to "take a deep breath" over + over! ♡

Day 45

I am grateful for your ability to withstand my criticism. Thank god.

46

I am grateful for your lack of self-consciousness — except for when I'm feeling self-conscious!

Day 47
My birthday

I am grateful for the ease...

the ease with which we interact...

your response to my desires "yes, dear" (!)

I feel like I can do whatever, whenever + you would continue to smile + support my wishes

Day 48

I am grateful for the "good vibrations" you give to me so lovingly.

Day 49

I am grateful for receiving the "oneness blessing" with you + then soaring together in dreamtime

Day 50

My darling, how grateful I am for your chivalry! At any time — even in night's midst — you handle whatever may be troubling me. (Last night it was the AC + clock) ♡

Day 51

I am oh-so-grateful for your willingness to take a walk with me on our Island's new bike path!

Nature + Glenn = my perfect combo

I love you!

Day 52

I love when you fully enjoy a meal I've created with love — this morning eggs with Opah, after ½ avocado (perfectly ripe) + apple slices.

Yummy - you are!

♡

Day 53

I am grateful for the ease with which you welcome friends – old & new – into our home & into our lives. You are so gracious & generous!

Tonight we entertained Marian & Louie, Darleen & Bruce + Kim, Carolyn + John at Hale Aloha. ♡

Day 54

My dear Glenn,

You boundless energy for handling so many things invisibly astounds me. I am grateful for your internal fortitude that does not seem to require acknowledgment from others (including me!) ♡

Day 55
I am grateful for your Presence.

Day 56

I am grateful for your willingness to work hard & finish a job well done – today we cleaned up Papalaea Cove with neighbors & friends, hauling wood debris for 4+ hours.

I love you ♡

Day 57

I am grateful for your BBQ culinary skills—tonite a rack of lamb yum! ♡

National Service Day 58

(see day 56 - oops! must be a couple of days behind)

Thank you for accepting me just as I am!

♡

Obama's Inauguration
Jan 20

Thank you, darling, for the personal climax to this magnificent, historic day.

I love you.

Day 60

I am grateful for your willingness to serve with non-attachment.

Will you continue to be President of the Lanikai Board? We will know soon!

♡

Day 61

I am grateful for your embrace. You are my resting place.

♡

We are halfway through the one hundred twenty-two entries in my gratitude journal. Rather than turning this little book into a tome by including the other sixty-one journal pages, I would prefer to share the remaining entries with you one at a time via a daily email. To receive them, simply enter your email address at www.GratitudeJournalNow.com.

Although I wrote my gratitude on only 122 days out of 365 that year, it was enough to save my marriage and give us years of pleasure since. Now when people ask me, "What's the secret to your great relationship with your husband?" I can say with clarity and conviction:

Focusing on what I am grateful for about him.

To elucidate, I might add:

When I focus on what I'm grateful for about my spouse (or my son, friend, or associate), it builds a strong foundation. Then, when irritating things arise (as they inevitably will), they seem miniscule in comparison to where I have placed most of my attention.

Glenn and I move around a great deal. The last three years we have lived near our son in Colorado in the summers, near my mom in Florida in the fall, and at our home in Kauai in the winters. With all the change in our lives, there is at least one thing I can depend on:

Wherever we are, Glenn always chooses to keep my special gratitude journal on his nightstand.

I encourage you to start your own gratitude journal on whatever in your life needs a lift: perhaps one of your own relationships, a job, or some difficult challenge.

With your love and gratitude, you can release yourself from feeling victimized, free yourself from the burden of judgment, and shift into a perspective that supports the joy-filled life you deserve.

Revolutionary Agreements

In June 1985, I moved from Washington, DC to live with Glenn in Boulder. That very same month we met with a group of friends and colleagues to support each other in living our highest values in every aspect of our lives. We began developing a set of agreements to guide us. That group (dubbed Geneva Group) was still meeting monthly twenty years later when I wrote a book based on those agreements, entitled *Revolutionary Agreements: Twelve Ways to Transform Stress and Struggle into Freedom and Joy.*

I am grateful beyond words for the Geneva Group participants, who for decades practiced the Geneva Group Agreements that ultimately led to the *Revolutionary Agreements*. I am especially grateful I was able to apply the underlying principles years later to revitalize my marriage. The Agreements have been and continue to be the most valuable practice in Glenn's and my personal and professional lives.

The Agreement most reflected in the pages of my gratitude journal is:

I agree to see the best in myself and others.

Please accept my gift of a downloadable poster of these Agreements at www.FreePosterNow.com. May it serve you and those you love.

About Marian and Glenn

Marian Head is the award-winning author of *Revolutionary Agreements: Twelve Ways to Transform Stress and Struggle into Freedom and Joy.* She and her husband Glenn choose to live by a set of Agreements they initiated with other visionary leaders in 1985. Along with their colleagues, they have been teaching and modeling these Agreements with their families, work teams, business stakeholders, clients, and communities for decades.

Visionary author and speaker Barbara Marx Hubbard refers to Marian and Glenn as "Humanity's Model Co-creative Couple." Together they guide people, organizations, and movements to envision and create their desired future. Whether leading a top-ranked sales team, co-chairing a Leadership and Organizational Transformation graduate department, helping a Fortune 100 team clarify its values, or co-facilitating Global Forums of Spiritual and Parliamentary Leaders on Human Survival, they bring conscious agreements, love, and joy to all they do.

www.RevolutionaryChoices.com

www.ingramcontent.com/pod-product-compliance
Lightning Source LLC
Chambersburg PA
CBHW040209020526
44112CB00039B/2849

Gratitude Journal for a Healthy Marriage is both a love story and practical guide for reviving, creating, or maintaining healthy relationships. Head shares her journey from the brink of separation to the rejuvenation of her marriage through the simple act of writing a daily gratitude to her husband.

> "It felt like I had permission to read someone's diary (very exciting). It has a sense of intimacy, which I love. I'm now noticing where I may take relationships for granted in my life and how I can apply gratitude to save the day. An important book."
>
> Rev. Patrick Feren, Co-Spiritual Director
> Center for Spiritual Living Kauai

> "The author's honesty and vulnerability are beautiful and exemplary. The world will be richer with this positive example of what people can do when the going gets rough."
>
> Gale Arnold, President
> Radio Tierra

www.RevolutionaryChoices.com

Author
Marian Head

USA $12.99 Marriage/Relationships

PAIDEIA MONOGRAPHS

THE SECULARIZATION OF SCIENCE

HERMAN DOOYEWEERD